To my grandfather,
who left without a final “I love you”

Cover image by Juan Carlos Varela

Cover and book design by Lynn Else

Original Spanish title: *Milo y el ciclo de la vida*
Text: Andrea Moreno
Illustrator: Juan Carlos Varela

Published by Parramon Paidotribo, S.L., Spain

Library of Congress Control Number: 2023942410

ISBN 978-0-8091-0674-5 (hardcover)
ISBN 978-0-8091-8857-4 (e-book)

Published by Paulist Press
997 Macarthur Boulevard
Mahwah, New Jersey 07430
www.paulistpress.com

Printed and bound in China
by Dream Colour (Hong Kong) Printing Limited
Shenzhen, Guangdong
November 2023

Milo
and the Cycle of Life

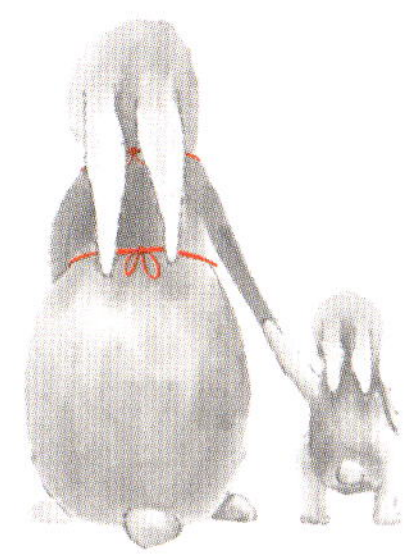

Andrea Moreno

ILLUSTRATIONS BY
Juan Carlos Varela

Paulist Press
New York / Mahwah, NJ

One autumn morning, Milo was hopping through the forest
when suddenly he felt a leaf falling on his nose.
He realized that the leaf, which used to be green
and fresh, was now brown and dry.
But...why? What caused this change?
Milo wondered thoughtfully.

He immediately returned to his burrow, looking for answers to all the questions that had arisen.

"Mom! Mom! You're not going to believe what happened to me! This leaf fell on my nose and look: it's brown and dry! Don't you think it's strange?"

His mother smiled. "Strange? We are in autumn, Milo. It's the cycle of life."

"The cycle of life?" asked Milo, confused.

"Come, I'll explain it to you."

“The life of the tree is reborn in spring. That’s when it needs the heat of the sun and the humidity of the forest to make its leaves grow. Like us, who need the warmth of our family to be cared for and protected.”

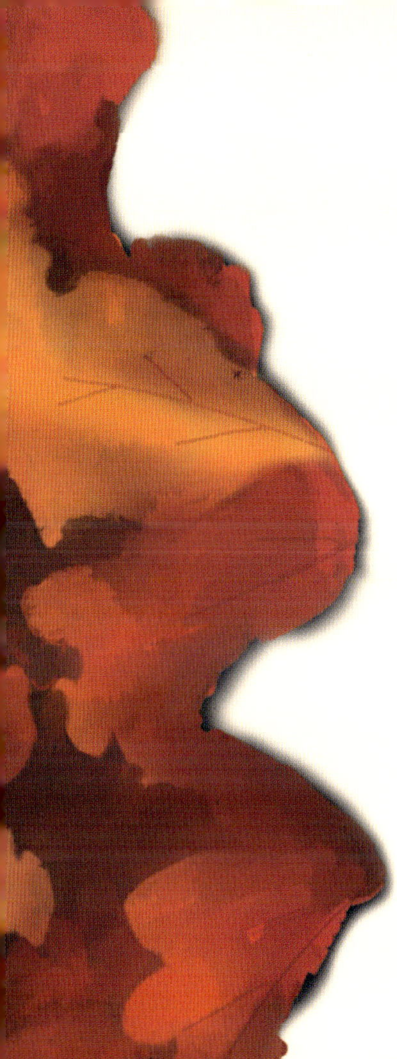

"After a while, the even warmer summer arrives. The tree is completely covered with leaves, beautiful, strong, green leaves."

"Wow, so many leaves! What a beautiful tree!" Milo exclaimed.

"That's right. Its many leaves make it more attractive than ever. Like us, as we grow, we become bigger and stronger. In the summer, the tree also grows fruit. Like us, who, when we are bigger, we have our babies."

"Like you, Mom, who had my little brothers and sisters and me."

"Exactly, Milo," Mom smiled.

"After a beautiful spring and a long summer, autumn arrives. We have already enjoyed the tree's fruits, and its leaves, now old, dry, and tired, begin to fall. But as these leaves fall, they will not disappear but will end up becoming part of the earth that feeds and helps the tree."

"So, the leaf that I kept, I should return it to the forest....Maybe the trees need it."

"That's a good idea, Milo, the trees will appreciate it. They will go through a long and cold winter, where they will look lonely and sad, but they are strong and wise. They need to rest and protect themselves from the cold so that they can bloom again with all their energy. Just like us, we also need time to feel better again after we lose someone we love."

"A time to…be sad?" asked Milo.

"And not just sad. Do you remember when grandpa died? How did you feel?"

"At first, I couldn't believe it, until we went to his burrow, and I realized that he wasn't there. Then I got very angry, because he left without saying goodbye. And I cried and cried because I wanted him to come back."

"And now, are you still sad?"

"Sometimes, yes, because I miss him. But I also like to remember the good times we spent together. And I laugh a lot hearing the stories that grandma tells about him."

"Of course, Milo. That's okay, but your anger and your sadness helped you to be able to remember him with affection and tenderness, and to feel how the love that united you will always be with you."

I love you,
Grandpa
milo

Milo thought for a moment and said, "I'll be right back, Mom," and he left the burrow. He walked through the forest until he reached the place where the leaf had fallen on him, and once again, he let it fall. And remembering what his mom had said, he looked within himself and spoke these most sincere words: "I love you, Grandpa."

The main idea of this story is based on a comparison between the life cycle of people and nature, according to the seasons of the year. This idea is originally from Xusa Serra, which she talks about in her book, *I jo, també em moriré?* (*And I, Will I Also Die?*).

This story is aimed at boys and girls from the age of four. Even so, the material is very flexible and can also be used with boys and girls of other ages, depending on the approach that is taken and what you want to focus on.

To get the most out of the story, you can consult the *Educational Guide* that is focused on teaching children ages four to six, with guidelines and ideas for activities to do.

To access the *Guide*, scan the following QR code: